NEW TO SYNCHRONIZED SWIMMING?

PARENTS—HERE IS YOUR GUIDE!

JACKIE ESKER ZERRUSEN

Balboa Press books may be ordered through booksellers or by contacting:

Balboa Press
A Division of Hay House
1663 Liberty Drive
Bloomington, IN 47403
www.balboapress.com
1 (877) 407-4847

ISBN: 978-1-5043-9258-7 (sc)
978-1-5043-9259-4 (e)

Print information available on the last page.

Balboa Press rev. date: 10/27/2018

BALBOA
PRESS
A DIVISION OF HAY HOUSE

Contents

Acknowledgements and Photo Credits

I owe appreciation to the coaches, parents, and swimmers who provided invaluable advice to me throughout the years. I could not have finished this book without the help of local coaches and my fantastic proof readers, you know who you are. I thank you from the bottom of my heart. And to all the parents reading this book, learning the sport for the first time, thank you too.

Photos in the last chapter are provided by John Migliore with Migz Media Group.

Introduction

As a parent new to synchronized swimming, I wanted to support my daughter in her new adventure of learning the sport. But I didn't know where to turn. A Google search and an Amazon search only disclosed so much. That's why I decided to put this guidebook together – to help other parents. As a non-swimming family, until now, I searched for resources and found very little. I was starting at ground zero, so I hunted for information from speed swimming and other synchronized swimming families and coaches. I've compiled the information in a format for first time parents (based on what I have learned through my daughter's club). When I refer to first time parents in this guidebook, it is those family members or legal guardians who are supporting a child new to this sport.

Should your daughter try? My answer is "of course!" Especially, if your daughter danced, swam or participated in gymnastics or cheerleading, she will understand and enjoy this sport. For the sake of readability I have used "she" throughout this text; all pronouns used are meant to represent any synchronized swimmer whether male or female.

This guidebook is organized so that you do not have to read it straight through. For example, you can jump to the chapter on equipment if you don't understand the nose clips.

And I have to include my disclaimer. The information in my book is solely based on my experiences and I am not endorsing nor promoting any particular product.

Chapter 1

What is Synchronized Swimming?

Dictionary.com states synchronized swimming is "a sport growing out of water ballet in which swimmers, in solo, duet, and team efforts, complete various required figures by performing motions in relatively stationary positions, along with a freestyle competition, with the contestants synchronizing movements to music and being judged by body position, control, and the degree of difficulty of the moves."

My definition is a little different. I believe it's a team sport where girls swim "in sync" with each other and to the music (dancing in the water). Since I began writing this book, the name of this sport has changed to Artistic Swimming. Regardless of the name, this sport requires tremendous grace, core strength, flexibility, breath control, split-second timing, and endurance.

I want to provide some clarification as some terms are used multiple ways. A "club" is an organization that has synchronized swimming teams. Most clubs are non profits such as a YMCA organization and many have parent associations. The advantage of a club is that they can incorporate cross-training activities for all skill levels, from entry level to elite training. Parent associations may also be available for additional support and involvement.

"Team" has multiple uses. It can mean all the synchronized swimming teams in a club or it can also mean a group of girls, in the same age group, swimming a routine together.

For purposes of this guidebook, "team" is the group of girls swimming together and "club" is the over-arching organization the girls swim for.

Chapter 2

Team Sport

Synchronized swimming is a team sport. All team sports require dedication. Attendance at practices and meets is extremely important for each team member. How can they be synchronized if not all the team members are present and involved? Involvement includes practices, fundraisers, team outings, competitions, etc.

Being on a team requires teamwork. The Dictionary.com definition of teamwork is a "cooperative or coordinated effort on the part of a group of persons acting together as a team or in the interests of a common cause". Girls do learn to help each other and support each other; an invaluable life skill.

Attendance

Coaches require attendance at practices in order for the team to build and improve. When one person misses practice, the effects are much larger. The team cannot work on the lifts or patterns if some of the girls are missing. The whole team loses that important practice time.

Many clubs will set travel black out dates and require girls on the team to attend practices to prepare for competition. This is usually during meet season.

Chapter 3

Synchronized Swim Terms

There are different swimming strokes (or swimming styles), such as butterfly, backstroke, breaststroke, and freestyle. An example of one for synchronized swimming is sculling. These are done in laps. Laps are one girl at a time swimming from one end of the pool to the other and then back again using a particular stroke. Basic skills include the egg beater kick and the scull. Egg beater is a form of treading water. It is used to perform strokes. Scull is the hand movements to propel the body. Some commonly used sculls are support, standard, torpedo, split-arm, barrel, and paddle scull. Support scull is used most often. And it is used when performing upside down figures.

In addition to the strokes, athletes also have figures and routines to work on. Figures are stationary body positions and transitions in the water. These vary by age group. Examples of figures are barracuda, ballet leg, front walkover, etc. plus groups of figures. What I call a flip out of the water, is called a lift in synchronized swimming. A lift is when team members propel another teammate relatively high out of the water. There are three parts to the lift. The person on top is the flyer. There is a base and pushers. The flyer is held by the base; that in turn is propelled upward by the pushers.

In addition to training in water, there is land training. Practices usually include both land and water training. Practice on land includes a workout, flexibility and stretching, and land drills (usually on the pool deck). Practice in the water includes swim workouts, drills, figures and routines.

The difference between the land and water is significant. On land, a ballet poise is to use your left hand to turn right. Under water and upside down, it is the opposite. One overarching difference is that swimmers have nothing from which to push off; requiring exceptional core strength. Points are deducted in an event if a team member touches the floor (bottom) of the pool.

Some adults have a hard time with backbends and flips, but girls in synchronized swimming develop skills to do these (if they do not know how already).

Back flips on land correlate to flips in the water. How amazing flips look out of the water! The challenge of flipping in the water is so much greater versus on land. Each teammate must be in the appropriate place for a flip, to avoid contact.

The girls do look out for each other in and out of the water. The awareness that the coach stresses is important, as well as having each team member very focused when swimming. This helps to avoid unintended physical contact under water.

Part of land training can include Pilates; which is hard work and fun while working the correct muscles. Flexibility is very important in synchronized swimming and it implies all joints in the body (such as the hips, lower back, ankles, etc). Some examples are included here to provide a better picture of what is expected of your daughter. A split is when the legs are extended in opposite directions and in alignment with each other. Right, left, and middle splits are needed; which for some swimmers this can be a huge challenge. An over split is when the legs go higher than the average split (greater than 190 degrees), so that when the swimmer is upside down in the water in a split, it looks wide and flat.

A bridge is when the body forms an arch, supported by the hands and feet. It can also be called a backbend. A toe point is when the foot is extended and the toes are pointed (and curled). Ankle exercises are available as are toe exercises for swimmers to obtain the proper leg and foot extensions needed.

Chapter 4

Competitions

Competitions are called meets. I was confused when someone called it a meet. A swim meet is a competition between two or more teams. Competitions have routines such as solos, duets, teams, trios, and / or combinations (combo) and each routine is judged. A routine is a dance (or swim) to music in the water and can be classified as a Free Routine or a Technical Routine. Free routines are not restricted by the choice of music, content, or choreography; they may have any listed figures and / or strokes to music. Technical routines have required elements that must be choreographed to music.

For competitions, a team is comprised of 4-8 girls performing. Solo is one person, duet is two, and trio is three. A combo routine is made up of 4-10 people.

Meet locations rotate and are determined by USA Synchro (more on that organization in chapter 6).

Different competitions that your swimmer may participate in are an Invitational, Association Meet, Regional Meet, Zone Meet, Junior Olympics, U.S. Nationals, and International competitions. Check with your daughter's team to find out which meets she will attend.

Junior Olympics is a national competition. The United States is split into four zones (East, West, North, South); which are then divided further into regions. East Zone has four regions. Winning a region qualifies a team for the national competition.

There are different age levels and skill levels: intermediate, age group, junior, senior, collegiate, and masters. Intermediate is for beginners, who are not as competitive. Solos, duets, trios, and team are performed at this level. Age group is the next level and is competitive. Solos, duets, team and combo are also performed at this more competitive level. Age groups are stratified age 12 and under, age 13 to 15, age 16 to 17, and age 18 to 19. Juniors and Seniors are more elite, more serious and much more competitive. Collegiate is for those swimmers who are completing on a team at a university. Masters is for those swimmers who have aged out, retired from competition but still want to enjoy the sport.

10 and Under	Intermediate
12 and Under	Intermediate or Age Group
13 and Over	Intermediate
13-15	Age Group
16-17	Juniors and Age Group
18-19	Seniors and Age Group
Collegiate	College / University level
Masters	Those aged out of competitions

Judging

The judges at meets have been trained. Judging positions are not paid, most are volunteer. Please keep that in mind. There are different types of judges with different types of training (should you decide to be a judge!). The levels are listed below. Technical routines (Level 3 and 4 below) have judges who judge on execution and overall impression. Free routines (Level 3 and 4 below) are judged on technical merit and artistic impression. Please refer to FINA (world governing body for aquatics, more details can be found in Chapter 9, Professional Organization) resources for further information. I've included a chart below for those who prefer to read it in a table format.

Level 1	12 and Under Age Group
Level 1F	12 and Under Age Group Figures
Level 2	Association / Regional
Level 2F	Association / Regional Figures
Level 3	Zone and Collegiate Regional (free routines and all technical routines)
Level 3F	Zone and Collegiate Regional Figures
Level 4	Zone and Collegiate Regional (free routines and all technical routines)
Level 4F	Zone and Collegiate Regional Figures

Other jobs at meets are timers, runners, announcers, music, concessions, etc. Volunteer requirements at a synchronized swimming meet can be different by club and/or team. Please check with your team for the specific details, as this list is not all inclusive. Some meets move rather quickly and some do not. As a spectator or a volunteer at a meet, be prepared for some downtime as well as the unexpected schedule change.

The first job I will mention is a timer. In the beginning, I could not understand why a timer was needed (much less three of them). Timers are volunteers who track time with a stop watch on the pool deck in full view of the competition. These timers keep track of the deckwork, starting with the opening sound of the music, and also the routine, until the final note of the music. Deckwork is the movement outside the water on the area near the pool. Timing standards/guidelines were created and are critical to keep the event moving. Deckwork must be 10 seconds or less. The routine, deckwork plus the whole music/time in water, is less than 3 minutes. Please note these guidelines are relevant at the time of this book writing and they also vary by age group and skill level.

The next job is a Runner. Runners pick up the judge's scoring slips and deliver them as quickly as possible to the on-deck scoring table. Runners will also pick up the timing slips from the timers. All slips are brought to the scoring table where data is entered into a computer program to determine the winners. A preliminary score is usually announced after the routine is finished. Final scores are posted and then the top finishers are usually announced during awards. In regards to the actual scoring, I'm still learning that; which is why I don't have further details.

Sound System

Each routine is announced over the loud speaker system at the competition. One or two volunteers handle the task of announcing routines and the girls' names.

Each team brings their own music (one song per routine) to the competition. One person is starting and stopping the music for each routine, as only one sound system is used.

Can the girls really hear the music under water? Just how does the music work?

Dancing in the water without music just couldn't happen. These are girls. They love music. The underwater sound system provides the beat to the swimmers in the water and to everyone out of the water.

Concessions

Concessions are a great fundraiser during meets. Cash payment for snacks, drinks (hot and cold), hot food (such as lasagna) or salads and sandwiches. Volunteers may be needed to purchase items in advance or to sell the products the day of the meet.

Attire for Meets

Coaches, teams, and judges all have certain clothing required for meets. Judges will wear a white shirt with black bottoms. Teams want to look the same, have that team look and feel to them. An intermediate team may not be as competitive, and may only wear team shorts and a shirt. These are usually purchased in advance of the season. Teams in the Age Group category may wear long pants, black flip flops, polo type shirts; also usually purchased in advance of the season. Coaches and team captains determine what clothing is worn and when. Team routines can have 4-8 girls all in the same swimsuit performing to music. Girls in solos, duets, trios have different suits from the team routine suits. There may be a rental cost or purchase price for performing suits and head pieces. More information can be found in the chapter on equipment under swim suits.

Chapter 5
Equipment

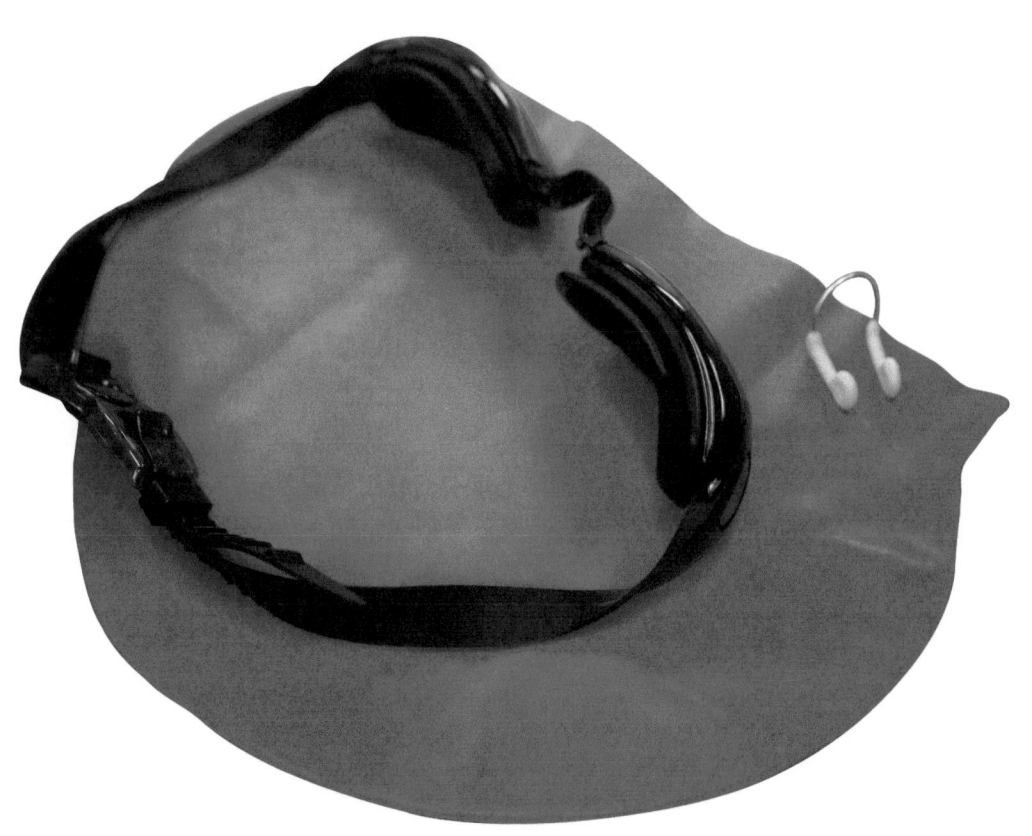

Swim Suits

Most sports require a uniform, and in synchro it's a swimsuit. But there are so many kinds. Starting out, who wants to purchase a $60 swimsuit if your daughter is not going to continue with the sport? Well, there is a reason for that price and it is worth the quality and headache of purchasing. But here are some points to keep in mind (that I wish I had known). Swimsuit should be a one piece, not a two piece.

Bathing suit straps must not restrict back and shoulder movement. Good swim suit stores can help with the fitting. Then you can buy online once you know the size as they are not the standard children sizes. Be prepared for the sizing. Suits are tight! If she leans over and there is a gap in the chest area, the suit is too big. When the suit is on the girl, the shoulder straps should not be able to be stretched up to the ears. If it stretches that far, the suit is too big. Some girls like the thin straps, less restriction makes you faster. My daughter preferred the thicker straps in the beginning, but now the thinner straps are more comfortable for her.

Yes, a good suit may cost $65 or more. Sale suits are usually half price. If you want the swimsuit to last, then the material is important. A polyester material will last longer. Spandex Lycra is less expensive but does not have a long life (material stretches too much too fast and becomes loose). We finally found the best fit for my daughter, regardless of material. Now that I know what she likes, I do purchase online (through swimoutlet.com) at a discount. I pinch pennies wherever I can; as this is an expensive sport!

Shorts can be worn with the bathing suit for land exercises, and then she can quickly enter the water just by taking her shorts off.

During competitions, your swimmer will wear a "costume"; which is a swim suit that matches the other girls performing the routine along with a head piece that matches the swim suit. The head piece is pinned onto each girl's head above her bun (in the same spot so they match).

One important tip is to take care of the costume. Team swim suits may have a lot of "bling" on them, as well as the headpiece. These sparkles will wear off if a washing machine is used. Most performance suits do not have machine washing or drying permitted. They are all rinsed in cold water and laid flat to dry. The head piece must be rinsed as well and laid flat to dry.

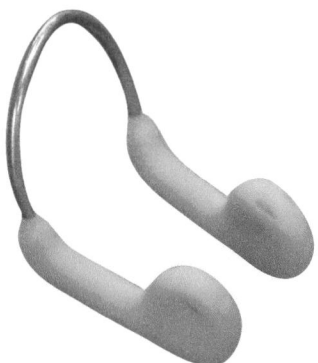

Nose Clips

Nose clips are important, so that water does not go up the nose when she is upside down in the water. Nose clips are adjustable. Prices, believe it or not, vary from $1 to over $3. There are multiple sizes but each one can be adjusted. And they sometimes leave a mark on the side of the nose; which can be healed with crème (we use "Arnica" gel). The nose clip fits right over the big part of the nose and squeezes the sides for a good fit. Be sure to have multiple nose clips on hand. Girls hook these extras onto their swimsuit, either at the hip or the shoulder strap. If the nose clip falls off in the water while she is performing, she can quickly replace it without having to stop.

Goggles

Goggles are great to see under water, to avoid hitting each other during practice. Opening eyes under water can be irritating. Although girls must perform without goggles at meets, dropping cold milk into the eyes is a great trick to soothe the irritation. "Speedo" and "Sporti" are two favorite brands for my daughter.

Mirrored goggles are probably too dark for indoor swimming but great for outdoor. The straps do break so extra straps on hand or extra goggles are a must. Girls wear white or clear goggles when they perform figures at meets. Check with your coach before purchasing new goggles, as the requirements may have changed.

Swim Caps

Caps are worn during practices and also at meets. Most teams wear their team caps during warm-ups at swim meets. Synchronized swimmers cannot wear caps for the actual competition; the hair is gelled back, which is discussed next.

Swim caps keep the hair up and in and somewhat dry. A cap is a latex or silicone covering on the girl's head; some put it over their ears too. Swimmers will tell you that the silicone caps are worth the extra money. Most teams have swim caps with their team logo. White swim caps are needed for a girl to compete in Figures at Meets.

Putting a swim cap on the first time is challenging. Other swimmers helped my daughter learn how. It is best to have a helper, the one wanting to wear the cap holds the cap tight to the forehead, then has the partner pull it high and hard over her head and release it down. Hopefully it doesn't snap down and cause a small reaction (or maybe that happens for fun).

Gel

Gelling (otherwise referred to as "Knoxing") at meets is an important task for swimmers and chaperones (discussed in chapter 4). To gel (or to 'Knox') means to pull girls' hair back with a gel so that it does not move in the water (stays back away from the face). The gelatin is clear (the consistency can vary from watery to thick and gooey) and it is painted on after the hair is pulled back, usually into a high bun. The bun itself does not require gel. Head pieces are then pinned on as the gel is drying. The drying time is less than a half hour.

Recommended gelling and other hair supplies are the "Knox" brand no flavor gelatin, bobby pins, hair nets, pony tail holders, small tooth comb, medium sized paint brush, small cup, and the head piece. The head piece is part of the costume and may be provided by the team. All other supplies must be purchased for each swimmer. Hair nets are tied around the bun, to keep the hair in the bun in one place. Bobby pins are used to hold the hair net and the bun and also the head piece. The goal is for the hair and the head piece to not move while the swimmer is in the water. This could take 30 to 50 (or more) bobby pins.

As a parent, the first time I saw someone gelling, I was shocked. And I asked myself, "why did I ever cook with that?" And "how does it come out?"

Remember those long hot showers your swimmer enjoys….that seems to be the best way to take the gel out. Rinse the hair with hot water and apply conditioner. Hot water, fingers and a wide tooth comb work best. We always find more gel the day after a meet; rarely is it ever out the first try.

Drinks

Girls must stay hydrated. Water is the best source. Water bottles can be kept by the pool, but check with your facility for material restrictions. There are insulated water bottles to keep water warm or cold, pending swimmer preference. Carbonated beverages hinder the girls from holding their breath longer under water and are not recommended. If a girl is dehydrated, her performance can suffer and she may not focus as well during practice and during meets. Hydration is so important. Please make sure your swimmer's water bottle is full (and she is drinking).

Towels

I always put beach towels away after summer because we don't go to the beach anymore. However, with a child who swims year round, I now have to have pool towels year round. Large beach towels or large bath towels work best for my daughter, but she also loves having a "shammy" towel for her hair. Special hair drying towels are available too. "Sporti" has a micro fiber dry towel; which my daughter likes and there are various pillowcase for wet heads available (which we have not tried). Pants can be found in a towel material. Whatever works for your swimmer, so she is warm and happy after swimming. Do not let the wet towel remain in the swim bag for too long – the smell is not pleasant.

Bag

Many swimmers use backpacks to carry all their supplies versus a duffel bag. Having a water proof bag is nice, but we have found that it's the compartments that matter most. The wet towel and swimsuit can be separated from the "dry" items. The wet items do cause a smell if they are left in the bag for too long. Expensive bags can be cleaned of the mildew, but better to not get to that point. The wet items should be taken out of the bag as soon as the swimmer arrives home after practice. Some teams will provide a team bag. Our team bag can only be used for meets; therefore another bag is needed for practices.

Other Equipment

Other equipment may be needed for training. Fins, ankle weights, jump ropes, and yoga mats are some possible training items. Fins are used to help improve swimming technique and ankle flexibility. Using ankle weights during a swim will build up muscle strength. Jumping rope is great conditioning. Yoga mats are used for stretching on a softer surface. Check with the coach for all the training items that will be needed, as these are just some examples.

Chapter 6
Miscellaneous

Locker Rooms

Locker rooms can be for adults only, kids, families or a combination of these. Be aware that locker rooms may be used for multiple sports and teams could finish practice at the same time.

There is no place for electronics in a locker room. Please stress to all athletes in locker rooms – the music, pictures, videos, texting, calling – all of these can wait.

Check the policies of your team and / or the club. Some require the swimmer's bag remain with the swimmer at all times (not left in the locker room).

Waiting – that's exactly what you do do after practice. Lots of girls rinsing and / or showering does take time. If your swimmer enjoys hot showers, discuss with her in advance how much time she can take. There could be more girls than shower stalls and locker rooms can be crowded. Be sure your swimmer understands your limits.

Showers

Showering after practice lets the chlorine smell stay at the club/pool versus traveling to your home/vehicle. Some girls prefer flip flops in the shower instead of being barefoot. Some girls just rinse off at the club and shower at home. Others will shower at the club, scrubbing, shampooing, etc., to not bring that smell home.

Chlorine can change the color of your hair. One day you look at the swimmer's hair and wonder why there is a tint of green in it (and not from her coloring it, but from swimming). Special shampoos are available to rid the chlorine from the hair. "Ultra Swim" is my daughter's favorite brand of chlorine removal shampoo.

Shoes and Feet

Land training is easiest in sneakers, to have a better grip. Water shoes may work best on the side of the pool. Flip flops or easy on and easy off shoes are the best, but they must be comfortable ones! Plain black flip flops are needed for meets.

As a parent, I shiver at the thought of all those bare feet and germs. If you stress sanitary conditions at home, she will be able to do it at the pool.

Toe nails and fingernails cannot be painted for competition. Groomed feet and trimmed nails are needed. When swimmers are upside down, their feet are visible out of the water. People are looking at the legs and feet.

Toes are always pointed. To help point their toes, (to me it looks like curling their toes), there are toe bands and sponges. Toe bands are thick black bands about 1 or 2 inches wide that hold the toe pointed, and wrap around the ankle. (Sounds so uncomfortable!) They are usually only used during practices, both in water and on land. Sponges are cut into long strips and toes are curled on them.

Coach

Your relationship with your daughter's coach is important. If something is going on with your girl at home or at school that may affect her performance at practice, I recommend sharing it with the coach. Some coaches do not want to have conversations with parents on the pool deck. Coaches do hold office hours for parents. The wait time after practice is a great time to speak to a coach – but sometimes coaches just want to go home after practice, so check with your swimming coach on the best times to talk.

Photographs

As part of the registration process, most teams require a photo permission and release form to be signed. Taking pictures creates great memories and is good for publicity. Some teams will create yearbooks at the season end. Please keep in mind this is a sport showing off legs. Pictures of legs in good synchro figures positions are great. Pictures of butts – not so great.

Water Temperature

Water temperature can vary by pool. Synchro teams use both outdoor and indoor pools. Indoor pools are not necessarily warm. Some Synchro teams wear a parka at meets, to keep them warm. Check with your team if your daughter does not have one. The parka is a huge thick coat, with a warm and fuzzy interior and a waterproof exterior. It has a hood and is very long. My first thought was why does she need this? I came to understand that at an outdoor pool in Florida. As soon as my daughter got out of the warm water, the cold wind felt freezing. The parka was wonderful!

Chapter 7
Obligations

There are different obligations with this sport and they can vary by club.

Financial

The first and probably the most important obligation is financial. There are club or organization fees, as well as pool fees and membership to USA Synchro. Additionally, each routine at a meet has an entry fee.

Parents can suddenly feel like their entire paychecks are going to the synchronized swimming sport.

Outfitting has costs also. This includes the team apparel, team swim suit and swim cap, routine swim suit and head piece, track suit, shorts, polo shirts, parka, backpack, etc. Check with the coach and / or the club for more details, as each team may handle financials differently.

Fundraising

Many teams fundraise to help offset the cost of the sport. Parents really need to be creative with fundraising ideas. Considering all the hidden costs that can come up with traveling to meets, it is a great idea to fundraise to offset those expenses.

Time

Another obligation is with time. There can be a big time commitment for the parent/guardian. If your swimmer is required to be in the pool 3 or 4 days a week, then you are driving her to and from the pool. Carpooling is a great option or if the pool is located in the school, then your daughter is already there on a school day. What does it look like if you support your swimmer 100%? Practices are 3-4 hours each, at least 3 days a week. Each routine may require a separate practice, which means more pool time. Meets or competitions are not as frequent, maybe one per month in the spring, which is typically the meet season. But meets can be multiple day events and often require travel.

Chaperones

In regards to time, parents are usually asked to volunteer their time to chaperone. Chaperones, or adults watching over girls during competitions, have an important responsibility at meets. The chaperone job varies based on meet location (travel or not). These jobs and the requirements do vary, so please check the team policy. Adults may have to pass a background check. They will drive the girls to meets, be in charge of all the girls at the meet, and be the main point of contact for the team (between the coach and the parents). For our club this includes snacks and meal planning. It may also be part of volunteer requirements which vary by club. The time commitment as a chaperone often spans the entire meet: preparation before, travel to and from the meet, parent politics during the meet, plus miscellaneous details to be cleaned up after.

Chapter 8
Health

Paying attention to health and wellness is extremely important. A girl's physical body must be ready to perform that routine. Proper fuel is required to do this. As a parent, please make sure your swimmer is fueled. Her health may suffer if she is not. In addition to drinking water and non carbonated beverages (daily), the amount of protein and carbohydrates is important. I felt my daughter was going into carbohydrate overload, but after a four hour practice, she needs to refuel. The proper mix of fruits and vegetables along with protein and fiber is a must. My family rule is five fruits and vegetables daily. After swimming, my daughter will eat 1-2 servings of rice or quinoa with some meat (assuming she's had her 5 fruits and vegetables for the day).

Most practices allow for break time and/or snack time. Possible snack ideas we have tried are popcorn, cheese sticks, fruit and raw vegetables (already cut into bite sized pieces), pepperoni, vegetable wraps (already cut into bite sized pieces), crackers or pretzels with hummus, protein bars, or yogurt with granola.

Sore muscles and injuries must be discussed too. It seems as though every muscle is used in the sport of synchronized swimming. If your swimmer has sore muscles, make sure she is drinking enough water. There are many ways to alleviate sore muscles, such as stretching (again!), muscle rolling, muscle cream, etc. Muscle rolling is massaging your muscle with a foam roller. The muscle cream my daughter uses is "Arnica". Cold water is great for sore muscles. You may have heard of an "ice bath". For an active recovery, light exercise is needed to keep the muscles moving. Your swimmer needs to find a method that works best for her.

Injuries are handled differently. A medical professional and the coach should be involved. There is growing concern over concussions in many sports. Swimmers can take a baseline concussion test to help aid in recovery if a concussion ever happens.

Chapter 9
Professional Organization

There is a professional organization associated with the synchronized swimming sport.

The Mission Statement for USA Synchro is below along with the website. They handle the rules and guidelines that must be followed in order to compete.

> "USA Synchro is recognized by the United States Olympic Committee as the National Governing Body for the sport of synchronized swimming and by FINA as a constituent member of United States Aquatic Sports for participation in the Olympic Games. USA Synchro unites, promotes and inspires athletes to achieve sustained competitive and personal excellence in the women's Olympic sport of synchronized swimming."

> https://www.teamusa.org/USA-Synchronized-Swimming

The professional organization responsible for all the aquatic sports in which synchronized swimming is included is FINA, **Fédération Internationale de Natation**. They establish unified rules; encourage international relations and competitions, and so much more. Please go to their website for further details http://www.fina.org/ .

Competitions can include the Olympics and the United States is building up to have a greater presence on the U.S.A. team.

Junior Olympics, Olympics, and the National Team are all great opportunities for a synchronized swimmer to advance. Qualifying for the Junior Olympics (JO's) happens at the Regional Meet. Teams throughout the United States can qualify for JO's. For further information on qualification requirements, please visit the USA Synchro website.

The National Team competes at the Pan Am games and at other various events throughout the world. There is a separate qualification process called Trials to earn a spot on the National Team.

Once a swimmer graduates from high school, she can compete at the collegiate level. Synchronized swimming is an NCAA sport at some universities. Other colleges hold the sport at the "club" level. The USA Synchro website has further information about the Varsity (Collegiate) and Club level. Because this sport is still smaller (than basketball and football), there are not many scholarships available. But your daughter can earn a scholarship for her grades, and then compete on a team.

Be prepared for the extra training, travel, and clothing to participate in those. But to see your daughter work so hard towards a goal and make it – to see her in the Olympics or to be on the National Team; what an honor!

Chapter 10

Swimmers' Viewpoints

So far, I have given information from a parent objective. Included here are viewpoints from two swimmers. First, my daughter has her say in what a parent should know about the sport. I think I saved the best for the last chapter.

"What I wished my parents knew when I started synchronized swimming is how to get me to practices on time, how to gel, that it is an expensive sport, and that swimsuits must be tight fitting."

"Next, I really wish my mother knew more about gelling my hair."

I also asked a high school synchronized swimmer, who has been swimming since she was little, what she would tell someone who was interested in this sport. Alexandra Poteet, who has since graduated and will be swimming at the collegiate level, mentioned people management skills. "Teammates learn to connect with those you may not have otherwise. You cannot limit yourself to certain social groups, because they are your team and you build a friendship like no other. And if you are swimming and not happy, it could be the environment (club) and/or the coach. The coach makes a different in the sport and you may need a new one."

And -
"You can never have enough nose clips and gel!"

Chapter 11
Photos

All photos are credited to John Migliore with Migz Media Group. More photos are available on his website at http://www.migzmediagroup.com/

Conclusion

Having a child try a new sport is an adventure for the entire family. Understanding the sport and speaking intelligently about it to your swimmer is priceless!

When synchronized swimming is mentioned, I always think of those sculpted legs reaching high out of the water (yes, very artistic!). As you have seen, it is that and so much more.

I hope this book has provided a clearer picture of synchronized swimming for a first time parent (guardian). Please keep in mind that the information was written in this book based on my experiences and my research at a point in time. Some of the details may have changed. It is important to maintain that relationship with the coach and the club to stay updated. This is such a beautiful and amazing sport that must be shared! Best of luck to your swimmer!

About the Author

As a mother, Jackie encourages her children to try new activities. Her daughter tried synchronized swimming for the first time during a two week summer camp. And as they say, the rest is history. Jackie is the mother of a daughter who loves synchronized swimming and has a family who loves watching it as well.

Resources

USA Synchro Meet Managers Guide, FINA rules, Migz Media Group, various internet searches, parents and coaches

Printed in the United States
By Bookmasters